# INFORMATION

| ORGANIZATION NAME | |
|---|---|
| **Registration Details** | |
| **Address:** | |
| | |
| | |

| | | | |
|---|---|---|---|
| **Phone No.** | | **Email** | |
| **Fax No.** | | **Emergency No.** | |
| **Website** | | | |
| **Log Book Number** | | | |

| | | | |
|---|---|---|---|
| **Continued From Log Book:** | | **Continued To Log Book:** | |
| **Date Log Started:** | | **Date Log Ended:** | |

# NOTES

_____
_____
_____
_____
_____
_____
_____
_____

www.signatureplannerjournals.com
www.signatureplannerjournals.co.uk

# INDIVIDUAL REAL ESTATE LOG

| NAME: | | DATE: | |
|---|---|---|---|
| PHONE NUMBER: | | EMAIL: | |
| ADDRESS: | | | |
| BUDGET: | | DEPOSIT: | |

## PREFERRED LOCATION | PROPERTY NEEDS

- 
- 
- 
- 
- 
- 
- 
- 
- 

## SUITABLE PROPERTIES

Viewed
- ○
- ○
- ○
- ○
- ○
- ○
- ○
- ○

## NOTES

_____
_____
_____
_____
_____
_____

## PROPERTY SOLD | COSTS

| | Value | |
| | Sold For | |
| | Commission | |

# INDIVIDUAL REAL ESTATE LOG

| NAME: | | DATE: | |
|---|---|---|---|
| PHONE NUMBER: | | EMAIL: | |
| ADDRESS: | | | |
| BUDGET: | | DEPOSIT: | |

## PREFERRED LOCATION | PROPERTY NEEDS

- 
- 
- 
- 
- 
- 
- 
- 
- 

## SUITABLE PROPERTIES / DATE OF VIEWING

Viewed
- ○
- ○
- ○
- ○
- ○
- ○
- ○
- ○

## NOTES

## PROPERTY SOLD | COSTS

| | Value | |
| --- | --- | --- |
| | Sold For | |
| | Commission | |
| | | |
| | | |
| | | |
| | | |
| | | |

# INDIVIDUAL REAL ESTATE LOG

**NAME:**                          **DATE:**

**PHONE NUMBER:**            **EMAIL:**

**ADDRESS:**

**BUDGET:**                       **DEPOSIT:**

## PREFERRED LOCATION      PROPERTY NEEDS

| | | | |
|---|---|---|---|
| • | • | • | • |
| • | • | • | • |
| • | • | • | • |
| • | • | • | • |
| • | • | • | • |
| • | • | • | • |
| • | • | • | • |
| • | • | • | • |
| • | • | • | • |

## SUITABLE PROPERTIES

**Viewed**

○
○
○
○
○
○
○
○

## NOTES

_____
_____
_____
_____
_____

## PROPERTY SOLD          COSTS

| | Value | |
|---|---|---|
| | Sold For | |
| | Commission | |
| | | |
| | | |
| | | |
| | | |
| | | |

# INDIVIDUAL REAL ESTATE LOG

| NAME: | | DATE: | |
|---|---|---|---|
| PHONE NUMBER: | | EMAIL: | |
| ADDRESS: | | | |

| BUDGET: | | DEPOSIT: | |
|---|---|---|---|

## PREFERRED LOCATION | PROPERTY NEEDS

- 
- 
- 
- 
- 
- 
- 
- 
- 

**Viewed** — **SUITABLE PROPERTIES / DATE OF VIEWING**

○
○
○
○
○
○
○
○

## NOTES

_____
_____
_____
_____
_____

## PROPERTY SOLD | COSTS

| | Value | |
|---|---|---|
| | Sold For | |
| | Commission | |
| | | |
| | | |
| | | |
| | | |
| | | |

# INDIVIDUAL REAL ESTATE LOG

**NAME:**                 **DATE:**

**PHONE NUMBER:**        **EMAIL:**

**ADDRESS:**

**BUDGET:**               **DEPOSIT:**

## PREFERRED LOCATION | PROPERTY NEEDS

| | | | |
|---|---|---|---|
| • | • | • | • |
| • | • | • | • |
| • | • | • | • |
| • | • | • | • |
| • | • | • | • |
| • | • | • | • |
| • | • | • | • |
| • | • | • | • |
| • | • | • | • |

## SUITABLE PROPERTIES

| Viewed | |
|---|---|
| ○ | |
| ○ | |
| ○ | |
| ○ | |
| ○ | |
| ○ | |
| ○ | |
| ○ | |
| ○ | |

## NOTES

_____
_____
_____
_____
_____
_____

## PROPERTY SOLD | COSTS

| | | |
|---|---|---|
| | Value | |
| | Sold For | |
| | Commission | |
| | | |
| | | |
| | | |
| | | |
| | | |

# INDIVIDUAL REAL ESTATE LOG

**NAME:**  
**DATE:**  
**PHONE NUMBER:**  
**EMAIL:**  
**ADDRESS:**  

**BUDGET:**  
**DEPOSIT:**  

## PREFERRED LOCATION | PROPERTY NEEDS

| PREFERRED LOCATION | | PROPERTY NEEDS | |
|---|---|---|---|
| • | • | • | • |
| • | • | • | • |
| • | • | • | • |
| • | • | • | • |
| • | • | • | • |
| • | • | • | • |
| • | • | • | • |
| • | • | • | • |

## SUITABLE PROPERTIES / DATE OF VIEWING

| Viewed | |
|---|---|
| ○ | |
| ○ | |
| ○ | |
| ○ | |
| ○ | |
| ○ | |
| ○ | |
| ○ | |

## NOTES

_____
_____
_____
_____
_____
_____

## PROPERTY SOLD | COSTS

| PROPERTY SOLD | | COSTS |
|---|---|---|
| | Value | |
| | Sold For | |
| | Commission | |
| | | |
| | | |
| | | |
| | | |
| | | |

# INDIVIDUAL REAL ESTATE LOG

NAME: DATE:

PHONE NUMBER: EMAIL:

ADDRESS:

BUDGET: DEPOSIT:

## PREFERRED LOCATION | PROPERTY NEEDS

- 
- 
- 
- 
- 
- 
- 
- 
- 

## SUITABLE PROPERTIES

Viewed
- ○
- ○
- ○
- ○
- ○
- ○
- ○
- ○

## NOTES

_____
_____
_____
_____
_____
_____

## PROPERTY SOLD | COSTS

| | Value | |
| --- | --- | --- |
| | Sold For | |
| | Commission | |

# INDIVIDUAL REAL ESTATE LOG

**NAME:**  
**DATE:**  
**PHONE NUMBER:**  
**EMAIL:**  
**ADDRESS:**  

**BUDGET:**  
**DEPOSIT:**  

## PREFERRED LOCATION | PROPERTY NEEDS

| PREFERRED LOCATION | | PROPERTY NEEDS | |
|---|---|---|---|
| • | • | • | • |
| • | • | • | • |
| • | • | • | • |
| • | • | • | • |
| • | • | • | • |
| • | • | • | • |
| • | • | • | • |
| • | • | • | • |

## SUITABLE PROPERTIES / DATE OF VIEWING

| Viewed | |
|---|---|
| ○ | |
| ○ | |
| ○ | |
| ○ | |
| ○ | |
| ○ | |
| ○ | |
| ○ | |

## NOTES

## PROPERTY SOLD | COSTS

| PROPERTY SOLD | | COSTS |
|---|---|---|
| | Value | |
| | Sold For | |
| | Commission | |
| | | |
| | | |
| | | |
| | | |

# INDIVIDUAL REAL ESTATE LOG

| NAME: | | DATE: | |
|---|---|---|---|
| PHONE NUMBER: | | EMAIL: | |
| ADDRESS: | | | |
| BUDGET: | | DEPOSIT: | |

## PREFERRED LOCATION | PROPERTY NEEDS

- 
- 
- 
- 
- 
- 
- 
- 
- 

## SUITABLE PROPERTIES

Viewed
- ○
- ○
- ○
- ○
- ○
- ○
- ○
- ○

## NOTES

_____
_____
_____
_____
_____

## PROPERTY SOLD | COSTS

| | Value | |
| | Sold For | |
| | Commission | |

# INDIVIDUAL REAL ESTATE LOG

| NAME: | | DATE: | |
|---|---|---|---|
| PHONE NUMBER: | | EMAIL: | |
| ADDRESS: | | | |
| BUDGET: | | DEPOSIT: | |

## PREFERRED LOCATION | PROPERTY NEEDS

| | | | |
|---|---|---|---|
| • | • | • | • |
| • | • | • | • |
| • | • | • | • |
| • | • | • | • |
| • | • | • | • |
| • | • | • | • |
| • | • | • | • |
| • | • | • | • |

## SUITABLE PROPERTIES / DATE OF VIEWING

| Viewed | |
|---|---|
| ○ | |
| ○ | |
| ○ | |
| ○ | |
| ○ | |
| ○ | |
| ○ | |
| ○ | |

## NOTES

_____
_____
_____
_____
_____
_____

## PROPERTY SOLD | COSTS

| PROPERTY SOLD | | |
|---|---|---|
| | Value | |
| | Sold For | |
| | Commission | |
| | | |
| | | |
| | | |
| | | |
| | | |

# INDIVIDUAL REAL ESTATE LOG

| NAME: | | DATE: | |
|---|---|---|---|
| PHONE NUMBER: | | EMAIL: | |
| ADDRESS: | | | |

| BUDGET: | | DEPOSIT: | |
|---|---|---|---|

## PREFERRED LOCATION | PROPERTY NEEDS

- 
- 
- 
- 
- 
- 
- 
- 
- 

## SUITABLE PROPERTIES

Viewed
- ○
- ○
- ○
- ○
- ○
- ○
- ○
- ○

## NOTES

---

## PROPERTY SOLD | COSTS

| Value | |
|---|---|
| Sold For | |
| Commission | |

# INDIVIDUAL REAL ESTATE LOG

**NAME:** 
**DATE:** 

**PHONE NUMBER:** 
**EMAIL:** 

**ADDRESS:** 

**BUDGET:** 
**DEPOSIT:** 

## PREFERRED LOCATION | PROPERTY NEEDS

| | | | |
|---|---|---|---|
| • | • | • | • |
| • | • | • | • |
| • | • | • | • |
| • | • | • | • |
| • | • | • | • |
| • | • | • | • |
| • | • | • | • |
| • | • | • | • |

## SUITABLE PROPERTIES / DATE OF VIEWING

| Viewed | |
|---|---|
| ○ | |
| ○ | |
| ○ | |
| ○ | |
| ○ | |
| ○ | |
| ○ | |
| ○ | |

## NOTES

_____
_____
_____
_____
_____
_____

## PROPERTY SOLD | COSTS

| | | |
|---|---|---|
| | Value | |
| | Sold For | |
| | Commission | |
| | | |
| | | |
| | | |
| | | |
| | | |

# INDIVIDUAL REAL ESTATE LOG

| NAME: | | DATE: | |
|---|---|---|---|
| PHONE NUMBER: | | EMAIL: | |
| ADDRESS: | | | |

| BUDGET: | | DEPOSIT: | |
|---|---|---|---|

## PREFERRED LOCATION | PROPERTY NEEDS

| | | | |
|---|---|---|---|
| • | • | • | • |
| • | • | • | • |
| • | • | • | • |
| • | • | • | • |
| • | • | • | • |
| • | • | • | • |
| • | • | • | • |
| • | • | • | • |
| • | • | • | • |

## SUITABLE PROPERTIES

| Viewed | |
|---|---|
| ○ | |
| ○ | |
| ○ | |
| ○ | |
| ○ | |
| ○ | |
| ○ | |
| ○ | |
| ○ | |

## NOTES

_____
_____
_____
_____
_____

## PROPERTY SOLD | COSTS

| | | |
|---|---|---|
| | Value | |
| | Sold For | |
| | Commission | |
| | | |
| | | |
| | | |
| | | |

# INDIVIDUAL REAL ESTATE LOG

**NAME:**  
**DATE:**  
**PHONE NUMBER:**  
**EMAIL:**  
**ADDRESS:**  

**BUDGET:**  
**DEPOSIT:**  

## PREFERRED LOCATION | PROPERTY NEEDS

- 
- 
- 
- 
- 
- 
- 
- 

## SUITABLE PROPERTIES / DATE OF VIEWING

| Viewed | |
|---|---|
| ○ | |
| ○ | |
| ○ | |
| ○ | |
| ○ | |
| ○ | |
| ○ | |
| ○ | |

## NOTES

## PROPERTY SOLD | COSTS

| | Value | |
|---|---|---|
| | Sold For | |
| | Commission | |
| | | |
| | | |
| | | |
| | | |
| | | |

# INDIVIDUAL REAL ESTATE LOG

| NAME: | | DATE: | |
|---|---|---|---|
| PHONE NUMBER: | | EMAIL: | |
| ADDRESS: | | | |
| BUDGET: | | DEPOSIT: | |

## PREFERRED LOCATION | PROPERTY NEEDS

- 
- 
- 
- 
- 
- 
- 
- 
- 

## SUITABLE PROPERTIES

Viewed
- ○
- ○
- ○
- ○
- ○
- ○
- ○
- ○
- ○

## NOTES

_____
_____
_____
_____
_____
_____
_____

## PROPERTY SOLD | COSTS

| | Value | |
| | Sold For | |
| | Commission | |

# INDIVIDUAL REAL ESTATE LOG

| NAME: | | DATE: | |
|---|---|---|---|
| PHONE NUMBER: | | EMAIL: | |
| ADDRESS: | | | |
| BUDGET: | | DEPOSIT: | |

## PREFERRED LOCATION | PROPERTY NEEDS

- 
- 
- 
- 
- 
- 
- 
- 

## SUITABLE PROPERTIES / DATE OF VIEWING

Viewed
- ○
- ○
- ○
- ○
- ○
- ○
- ○
- ○

## NOTES

_____
_____
_____
_____
_____

## PROPERTY SOLD | COSTS

| | Value | |
| | Sold For | |
| | Commission | |

# INDIVIDUAL REAL ESTATE LOG

| NAME: | | DATE: | |
|---|---|---|---|
| PHONE NUMBER: | | EMAIL: | |
| ADDRESS: | | | |

| BUDGET: | | DEPOSIT: | |
|---|---|---|---|

## PREFERRED LOCATION | PROPERTY NEEDS

| | | | |
|---|---|---|---|
| • | • | • | • |
| • | • | • | • |
| • | • | • | • |
| • | • | • | • |
| • | • | • | • |
| • | • | • | • |
| • | • | • | • |
| • | • | • | • |
| • | • | • | • |

## SUITABLE PROPERTIES

| Viewed | |
|---|---|
| ○ | |
| ○ | |
| ○ | |
| ○ | |
| ○ | |
| ○ | |
| ○ | |
| ○ | |

## NOTES

_____
_____
_____
_____
_____

## PROPERTY SOLD | COSTS

| | | |
|---|---|---|
| | Value | |
| | Sold For | |
| | Commission | |
| | | |
| | | |
| | | |
| | | |
| | | |

# INDIVIDUAL REAL ESTATE LOG

**NAME:** 
**DATE:** 
**PHONE NUMBER:** 
**EMAIL:** 
**ADDRESS:** 

**BUDGET:** 
**DEPOSIT:** 

## PREFERRED LOCATION | PROPERTY NEEDS

- 
- 
- 
- 
- 
- 
- 
- 
- 

## SUITABLE PROPERTIES / DATE OF VIEWING

Viewed
- ○
- ○
- ○
- ○
- ○
- ○
- ○
- ○

## NOTES

---

## PROPERTY SOLD | COSTS

| | |
|---|---|
| Value | |
| Sold For | |
| Commission | |
| | |
| | |
| | |
| | |
| | |

# INDIVIDUAL REAL ESTATE LOG

| NAME: | | DATE: | |
|---|---|---|---|
| PHONE NUMBER: | | EMAIL: | |
| ADDRESS: | | | |
| BUDGET: | | DEPOSIT: | |

## PREFERRED LOCATION | PROPERTY NEEDS

- 
- 
- 
- 
- 
- 
- 
- 
- 

## SUITABLE PROPERTIES

Viewed
- ○
- ○
- ○
- ○
- ○
- ○
- ○
- ○

## NOTES

_____
_____
_____
_____
_____
_____

## PROPERTY SOLD | COSTS

| | Value | |
|---|---|---|
| | Sold For | |
| | Commission | |
| | | |
| | | |
| | | |
| | | |

# INDIVIDUAL REAL ESTATE LOG

**NAME:**  
**DATE:**  
**PHONE NUMBER:**  
**EMAIL:**  
**ADDRESS:**  

**BUDGET:**  
**DEPOSIT:**

## PREFERRED LOCATION | PROPERTY NEEDS

- 
- 
- 
- 
- 
- 
- 
- 
- 

## SUITABLE PROPERTIES / DATE OF VIEWING

Viewed
- ○
- ○
- ○
- ○
- ○
- ○
- ○
- ○

## NOTES

_____
_____
_____
_____
_____

## PROPERTY SOLD | COSTS

| | |
|---|---|
| Value | |
| Sold For | |
| Commission | |
| | |
| | |
| | |
| | |
| | |

# INDIVIDUAL REAL ESTATE LOG

| NAME: | | DATE: | |
|---|---|---|---|
| PHONE NUMBER: | | EMAIL: | |
| ADDRESS: | | | |
| BUDGET: | | DEPOSIT: | |

## PREFERRED LOCATION | PROPERTY NEEDS

| Preferred Location | | Property Needs | |
|---|---|---|---|
| • | • | • | • |
| • | • | • | • |
| • | • | • | • |
| • | • | • | • |
| • | • | • | • |
| • | • | • | • |
| • | • | • | • |
| • | • | • | • |

## SUITABLE PROPERTIES

| Viewed | |
|---|---|
| ○ | |
| ○ | |
| ○ | |
| ○ | |
| ○ | |
| ○ | |
| ○ | |
| ○ | |

## NOTES

_____
_____
_____
_____
_____

## PROPERTY SOLD | COSTS

| Property Sold | | Costs |
|---|---|---|
| | Value | |
| | Sold For | |
| | Commission | |
| | | |
| | | |
| | | |
| | | |
| | | |

# INDIVIDUAL REAL ESTATE LOG

NAME: 
DATE: 

PHONE NUMBER: 
EMAIL: 

ADDRESS: 

BUDGET: 
DEPOSIT: 

## PREFERRED LOCATION | PROPERTY NEEDS

- 
- 
- 
- 
- 
- 
- 
- 
- 

## SUITABLE PROPERTIES / DATE OF VIEWING

Viewed
- ○
- ○
- ○
- ○
- ○
- ○
- ○
- ○

## NOTES

_____
_____
_____
_____
_____
_____

## PROPERTY SOLD | COSTS

| | |
|---|---|
| Value | |
| Sold For | |
| Commission | |
| | |
| | |
| | |
| | |
| | |

# INDIVIDUAL REAL ESTATE LOG

**NAME:**  
**DATE:**  
**PHONE NUMBER:**  
**EMAIL:**  
**ADDRESS:**  

**BUDGET:**  
**DEPOSIT:**  

## PREFERRED LOCATION | PROPERTY NEEDS

| Preferred Location | | Property Needs | |
|---|---|---|---|
| • | • | • | • |
| • | • | • | • |
| • | • | • | • |
| • | • | • | • |
| • | • | • | • |
| • | • | • | • |
| • | • | • | • |
| • | • | • | • |
| • | • | • | • |

## SUITABLE PROPERTIES

| Viewed | |
|---|---|
| ○ | |
| ○ | |
| ○ | |
| ○ | |
| ○ | |
| ○ | |
| ○ | |
| ○ | |

## NOTES

## PROPERTY SOLD | COSTS

| Property Sold | | | |
|---|---|---|---|
| | Value | | |
| | Sold For | | |
| | Commission | | |
| | | | |
| | | | |
| | | | |
| | | | |

# INDIVIDUAL REAL ESTATE LOG

**NAME:**　　　　　　　　　　　　　　　　**DATE:**

**PHONE NUMBER:**　　　　　　　　　　　**EMAIL:**

**ADDRESS:**

**BUDGET:**　　　　　　　　　　　　　　　**DEPOSIT:**

## PREFERRED LOCATION | PROPERTY NEEDS

| Preferred Location | | Property Needs | |
|---|---|---|---|
| • | • | • | • |
| • | • | • | • |
| • | • | • | • |
| • | • | • | • |
| • | • | • | • |
| • | • | • | • |
| • | • | • | • |
| • | • | • | • |

## SUITABLE PROPERTIES / DATE OF VIEWING

| Viewed | |
|---|---|
| ○ | |
| ○ | |
| ○ | |
| ○ | |
| ○ | |
| ○ | |
| ○ | |
| ○ | |

## NOTES

_____
_____
_____
_____
_____

## PROPERTY SOLD | COSTS

| Property Sold | | Costs |
|---|---|---|
| | Value | |
| | Sold For | |
| | Commission | |
| | | |
| | | |
| | | |
| | | |
| | | |

# INDIVIDUAL REAL ESTATE LOG

**NAME:**  
**DATE:**  
**PHONE NUMBER:**  
**EMAIL:**  
**ADDRESS:**  

**BUDGET:**  
**DEPOSIT:**

## PREFERRED LOCATION | PROPERTY NEEDS

| PREFERRED LOCATION | | PROPERTY NEEDS | |
|---|---|---|---|
| • | • | • | • |
| • | • | • | • |
| • | • | • | • |
| • | • | • | • |
| • | • | • | • |
| • | • | • | • |
| • | • | • | • |
| • | • | • | • |

## SUITABLE PROPERTIES

| Viewed | |
|---|---|
| ○ | |
| ○ | |
| ○ | |
| ○ | |
| ○ | |
| ○ | |
| ○ | |
| ○ | |

## NOTES

## PROPERTY SOLD | COSTS

| PROPERTY SOLD | | COSTS |
|---|---|---|
| | Value | |
| | Sold For | |
| | Commission | |
| | | |
| | | |
| | | |
| | | |
| | | |

# INDIVIDUAL REAL ESTATE LOG

**NAME:**  
**DATE:**  
**PHONE NUMBER:**  
**EMAIL:**  
**ADDRESS:**  

**BUDGET:**  
**DEPOSIT:**  

| PREFERRED LOCATION | | PROPERTY NEEDS | |
|---|---|---|---|
| • | • | • | • |
| • | • | • | • |
| • | • | • | • |
| • | • | • | • |
| • | • | • | • |
| • | • | • | • |
| • | • | • | • |
| • | • | • | • |

## SUITABLE PROPERTIES / DATE OF VIEWING

| Viewed | |
|---|---|
| ○ | |
| ○ | |
| ○ | |
| ○ | |
| ○ | |
| ○ | |
| ○ | |
| ○ | |

## NOTES

_____
_____
_____
_____
_____
_____

| PROPERTY SOLD | | COSTS |
|---|---|---|
| | Value | |
| | Sold For | |
| | Commission | |
| | | |
| | | |
| | | |
| | | |

# INDIVIDUAL REAL ESTATE LOG

| NAME: | | DATE: | |
|---|---|---|---|
| PHONE NUMBER: | | EMAIL: | |
| ADDRESS: | | | |

| BUDGET: | | DEPOSIT: | |
|---|---|---|---|

## PREFERRED LOCATION | PROPERTY NEEDS

- 
- 
- 
- 
- 
- 
- 
- 
- 

## SUITABLE PROPERTIES

Viewed
- ○
- ○
- ○
- ○
- ○
- ○
- ○
- ○

## NOTES

---

## PROPERTY SOLD | COSTS

| | Value | |
|---|---|---|
| | Sold For | |
| | Commission | |
| | | |
| | | |
| | | |
| | | |
| | | |

# INDIVIDUAL REAL ESTATE LOG

| NAME: | | DATE: | |
|---|---|---|---|
| PHONE NUMBER: | | EMAIL: | |
| ADDRESS: | | | |

| BUDGET: | | DEPOSIT: | |
|---|---|---|---|

## PREFERRED LOCATION | PROPERTY NEEDS

| | | | |
|---|---|---|---|
| • | • | • | • |
| • | • | • | • |
| • | • | • | • |
| • | • | • | • |
| • | • | • | • |
| • | • | • | • |
| • | • | • | • |
| • | • | • | • |

## SUITABLE PROPERTIES / DATE OF VIEWING

Viewed
- ○
- ○
- ○
- ○
- ○
- ○
- ○
- ○

## NOTES

_____
_____
_____
_____
_____
_____

## PROPERTY SOLD | COSTS

| | |
|---|---|
| Value | |
| Sold For | |
| Commission | |
| | |
| | |
| | |
| | |

# INDIVIDUAL REAL ESTATE LOG

NAME: _____          DATE: _____

PHONE NUMBER: _____  EMAIL: _____

ADDRESS: _____

BUDGET: _____        DEPOSIT: _____

## PREFERRED LOCATION | PROPERTY NEEDS

- 
- 
- 
- 
- 
- 
- 
- 
- 

## SUITABLE PROPERTIES

Viewed
- ○
- ○
- ○
- ○
- ○
- ○
- ○
- ○

## NOTES

_____
_____
_____
_____
_____
_____

## PROPERTY SOLD | COSTS

| | Value | |
| | Sold For | |
| | Commission | |

# INDIVIDUAL REAL ESTATE LOG

**NAME:**  
**DATE:**  
**PHONE NUMBER:**  
**EMAIL:**  
**ADDRESS:**  

**BUDGET:**  
**DEPOSIT:**

## PREFERRED LOCATION | PROPERTY NEEDS

| Preferred Location | | Property Needs | |
|---|---|---|---|
| • | • | • | • |
| • | • | • | • |
| • | • | • | • |
| • | • | • | • |
| • | • | • | • |
| • | • | • | • |
| • | • | • | • |
| • | • | • | • |

## SUITABLE PROPERTIES / DATE OF VIEWING

| Viewed | |
|---|---|
| ○ | |
| ○ | |
| ○ | |
| ○ | |
| ○ | |
| ○ | |
| ○ | |
| ○ | |

## NOTES

_____
_____
_____
_____
_____
_____

## PROPERTY SOLD | COSTS

| Property Sold | | Costs |
|---|---|---|
| | Value | |
| | Sold For | |
| | Commission | |
| | | |
| | | |
| | | |
| | | |
| | | |

# INDIVIDUAL REAL ESTATE LOG

| NAME: | | DATE: | |
|---|---|---|---|
| PHONE NUMBER: | | EMAIL: | |
| ADDRESS: | | | |

| BUDGET: | | DEPOSIT: | |
|---|---|---|---|

## PREFERRED LOCATION | PROPERTY NEEDS

| | | | |
|---|---|---|---|
| • | • | • | • |
| • | • | • | • |
| • | • | • | • |
| • | • | • | • |
| • | • | • | • |
| • | • | • | • |
| • | • | • | • |
| • | • | • | • |
| • | • | • | • |

### SUITABLE PROPERTIES

| Viewed | |
|---|---|
| ○ | |
| ○ | |
| ○ | |
| ○ | |
| ○ | |
| ○ | |
| ○ | |
| ○ | |
| ○ | |

## NOTES

_____
_____
_____
_____
_____

## PROPERTY SOLD | COSTS

| PROPERTY SOLD | | |
|---|---|---|
| | Value | |
| | Sold For | |
| | Commission | |
| | | |
| | | |
| | | |
| | | |
| | | |

# INDIVIDUAL REAL ESTATE LOG

NAME: _____    DATE: _____

PHONE NUMBER: _____    EMAIL: _____

ADDRESS: _____

BUDGET: _____    DEPOSIT: _____

| PREFERRED LOCATION | | PROPERTY NEEDS | |
|---|---|---|---|
| • | • | • | • |
| • | • | • | • |
| • | • | • | • |
| • | • | • | • |
| • | • | • | • |
| • | • | • | • |
| • | • | • | • |
| • | • | • | • |

## SUITABLE PROPERTIES / DATE OF VIEWING

Viewed
- ○
- ○
- ○
- ○
- ○
- ○
- ○
- ○

## NOTES

_____
_____
_____
_____
_____
_____

## PROPERTY SOLD | COSTS

| Value | |
| Sold For | |
| Commission | |

# INDIVIDUAL REAL ESTATE LOG

**NAME:**  
**DATE:**  
**PHONE NUMBER:**  
**EMAIL:**  
**ADDRESS:**  
**BUDGET:**  
**DEPOSIT:**

## PREFERRED LOCATION | PROPERTY NEEDS

- 
- 
- 
- 
- 
- 
- 
- 
- 

## SUITABLE PROPERTIES

Viewed
- ○
- ○
- ○
- ○
- ○
- ○
- ○
- ○

## NOTES

## PROPERTY SOLD | COSTS

| | |
|---|---|
| Value | |
| Sold For | |
| Commission | |

# INDIVIDUAL REAL ESTATE LOG

**NAME:**  
**PHONE NUMBER:**  
**ADDRESS:**  

**DATE:**  
**EMAIL:**  

**BUDGET:**  
**DEPOSIT:**  

## PREFERRED LOCATION | PROPERTY NEEDS

- 
- 
- 
- 
- 
- 
- 
- 

- 
- 
- 
- 
- 
- 
- 
- 

- 
- 
- 
- 
- 
- 
- 
- 

- 
- 
- 
- 
- 
- 
- 
- 

## SUITABLE PROPERTIES / DATE OF VIEWING

| Viewed | |
|---|---|
| ○ | |
| ○ | |
| ○ | |
| ○ | |
| ○ | |
| ○ | |
| ○ | |
| ○ | |

## NOTES

_____
_____
_____
_____
_____
_____

## PROPERTY SOLD | COSTS

| | Value | |
|---|---|---|
| | Sold For | |
| | Commission | |
| | | |
| | | |
| | | |
| | | |
| | | |

# INDIVIDUAL REAL ESTATE LOG

**NAME:**  
**DATE:**  
**PHONE NUMBER:**  
**EMAIL:**  
**ADDRESS:**  

**BUDGET:**  
**DEPOSIT:**

## PREFERRED LOCATION | PROPERTY NEEDS

| Preferred Location | | Property Needs | |
|---|---|---|---|
| • | • | • | • |
| • | • | • | • |
| • | • | • | • |
| • | • | • | • |
| • | • | • | • |
| • | • | • | • |
| • | • | • | • |
| • | • | • | • |
| • | • | • | • |

## SUITABLE PROPERTIES

| Viewed | |
|---|---|
| ○ | |
| ○ | |
| ○ | |
| ○ | |
| ○ | |
| ○ | |
| ○ | |
| ○ | |

## NOTES

## PROPERTY SOLD | COSTS

| Value | |
|---|---|
| Sold For | |
| Commission | |

# INDIVIDUAL REAL ESTATE LOG

NAME:                          DATE:

PHONE NUMBER:            EMAIL:

ADDRESS:

BUDGET:                    DEPOSIT:

## PREFERRED LOCATION | PROPERTY NEEDS

| | | | |
|---|---|---|---|
| • | • | • | • |
| • | • | • | • |
| • | • | • | • |
| • | • | • | • |
| • | • | • | • |
| • | • | • | • |
| • | • | • | • |
| • | • | • | • |
| • | • | • | • |

## SUITABLE PROPERTIES / DATE OF VIEWING

Viewed
- ○
- ○
- ○
- ○
- ○
- ○
- ○
- ○

## NOTES

_____
_____
_____
_____
_____
_____

## PROPERTY SOLD | COSTS

| | |
|---|---|
| Value | |
| Sold For | |
| Commission | |
| | |
| | |
| | |
| | |

# INDIVIDUAL REAL ESTATE LOG

| NAME: | | DATE: | |
|---|---|---|---|
| PHONE NUMBER: | | EMAIL: | |
| ADDRESS: | | | |

| BUDGET: | | DEPOSIT: | |
|---|---|---|---|

## PREFERRED LOCATION | PROPERTY NEEDS

| | | | |
|---|---|---|---|
| • | • | • | • |
| • | • | • | • |
| • | • | • | • |
| • | • | • | • |
| • | • | • | • |
| • | • | • | • |
| • | • | • | • |
| • | • | • | • |
| • | • | • | • |

## SUITABLE PROPERTIES

| Viewed | |
|---|---|
| ○ | |
| ○ | |
| ○ | |
| ○ | |
| ○ | |
| ○ | |
| ○ | |
| ○ | |
| ○ | |

## NOTES

_____
_____
_____
_____
_____
_____

## PROPERTY SOLD | COSTS

| | Value | |
|---|---|---|
| | Sold For | |
| | Commission | |
| | | |
| | | |
| | | |
| | | |

# INDIVIDUAL REAL ESTATE LOG

| NAME: | | DATE: | |
|---|---|---|---|
| PHONE NUMBER: | | EMAIL: | |
| ADDRESS: | | | |

| BUDGET: | | DEPOSIT: | |
|---|---|---|---|

## PREFERRED LOCATION | PROPERTY NEEDS

| • | • | • | • |
|---|---|---|---|
| • | • | • | • |
| • | • | • | • |
| • | • | • | • |
| • | • | • | • |
| • | • | • | • |
| • | • | • | • |
| • | • | • | • |

### Viewed — SUITABLE PROPERTIES/ DATE OF VIEWING

| Viewed | |
|---|---|
| ○ | |
| ○ | |
| ○ | |
| ○ | |
| ○ | |
| ○ | |
| ○ | |
| ○ | |

## NOTES

_____
_____
_____
_____
_____
_____

## PROPERTY SOLD | COSTS

| PROPERTY SOLD | | COSTS | |
|---|---|---|---|
| | Value | | |
| | Sold For | | |
| | Commission | | |
| | | | |
| | | | |
| | | | |
| | | | |
| | | | |

# INDIVIDUAL REAL ESTATE LOG

| NAME: | | DATE: | |
|---|---|---|---|
| PHONE NUMBER: | | EMAIL: | |
| ADDRESS: | | | |

| BUDGET: | | DEPOSIT: | |
|---|---|---|---|

| PREFERRED LOCATION | | PROPERTY NEEDS | |
|---|---|---|---|
| • | • | • | • |
| • | • | • | • |
| • | • | • | • |
| • | • | • | • |
| • | • | • | • |
| • | • | • | • |
| • | • | • | • |
| • | • | • | • |

## SUITABLE PROPERTIES

| Viewed | |
|---|---|
| ○ | |
| ○ | |
| ○ | |
| ○ | |
| ○ | |
| ○ | |
| ○ | |
| ○ | |
| ○ | |

## NOTES

_____
_____
_____
_____
_____
_____

| PROPERTY SOLD | | COSTS | |
|---|---|---|---|
| | Value | | |
| | Sold For | | |
| | Commission | | |
| | | | |
| | | | |
| | | | |
| | | | |

# INDIVIDUAL REAL ESTATE LOG

**NAME:** _____  **DATE:** _____

**PHONE NUMBER:** _____  **EMAIL:** _____

**ADDRESS:** _____

**BUDGET:** _____  **DEPOSIT:** _____

## PREFERRED LOCATION | PROPERTY NEEDS

| Preferred Location | | Property Needs | |
|---|---|---|---|
| • | • | • | • |
| • | • | • | • |
| • | • | • | • |
| • | • | • | • |
| • | • | • | • |
| • | • | • | • |
| • | • | • | • |
| • | • | • | • |

## SUITABLE PROPERTIES / DATE OF VIEWING

| Viewed | |
|---|---|
| ○ | |
| ○ | |
| ○ | |
| ○ | |
| ○ | |
| ○ | |
| ○ | |
| ○ | |

## NOTES

_____
_____
_____
_____
_____
_____

## PROPERTY SOLD | COSTS

| Property Sold | | Costs |
|---|---|---|
| | Value | |
| | Sold For | |
| | Commission | |
| | | |
| | | |
| | | |
| | | |

# INDIVIDUAL REAL ESTATE LOG

| NAME: | | DATE: | |
|---|---|---|---|
| PHONE NUMBER: | | EMAIL: | |
| ADDRESS: | | | |
| BUDGET: | | DEPOSIT: | |

## PREFERRED LOCATION | PROPERTY NEEDS

- 
- 
- 
- 
- 
- 
- 
- 
- 

## SUITABLE PROPERTIES

**Viewed**
- ○
- ○
- ○
- ○
- ○
- ○
- ○
- ○

## NOTES

_____
_____
_____
_____
_____

## PROPERTY SOLD | COSTS

| | Value | |
| | Sold For | |
| | Commission | |

# INDIVIDUAL REAL ESTATE LOG

| NAME: | | DATE: | |
|---|---|---|---|
| PHONE NUMBER: | | EMAIL: | |
| ADDRESS: | | | |
| BUDGET: | | DEPOSIT: | |

| PREFERRED LOCATION | | PROPERTY NEEDS | |
|---|---|---|---|
| • | • | • | • |
| • | • | • | • |
| • | • | • | • |
| • | • | • | • |
| • | • | • | • |
| • | • | • | • |
| • | • | • | • |
| • | • | • | • |

### Viewed — SUITABLE PROPERTIES / DATE OF VIEWING

| Viewed | |
|---|---|
| ○ | |
| ○ | |
| ○ | |
| ○ | |
| ○ | |
| ○ | |
| ○ | |
| ○ | |

## NOTES

_____
_____
_____
_____
_____
_____

| PROPERTY SOLD | | COSTS |
|---|---|---|
| | Value | |
| | Sold For | |
| | Commission | |
| | | |
| | | |
| | | |
| | | |
| | | |

# INDIVIDUAL REAL ESTATE LOG

| NAME: | | DATE: | |
|---|---|---|---|
| PHONE NUMBER: | | EMAIL: | |
| ADDRESS: | | | |
| BUDGET: | | DEPOSIT: | |

| PREFERRED LOCATION | | PROPERTY NEEDS | |
|---|---|---|---|
| • | • | • | • |
| • | • | • | • |
| • | • | • | • |
| • | • | • | • |
| • | • | • | • |
| • | • | • | • |
| • | • | • | • |
| • | • | • | • |

## SUITABLE PROPERTIES

| Viewed | |
|---|---|
| ○ | |
| ○ | |
| ○ | |
| ○ | |
| ○ | |
| ○ | |
| ○ | |
| ○ | |

## NOTES

_____
_____
_____
_____
_____
_____

| PROPERTY SOLD | | COSTS | |
|---|---|---|---|
| | Value | | |
| | Sold For | | |
| | Commission | | |
| | | | |
| | | | |
| | | | |
| | | | |

# INDIVIDUAL REAL ESTATE LOG

**NAME:**  
**PHONE NUMBER:**  
**ADDRESS:**  
**DATE:**  
**EMAIL:**  
**BUDGET:**  
**DEPOSIT:**

## PREFERRED LOCATION | PROPERTY NEEDS

- 
- 
- 
- 
- 
- 
- 
- 

## SUITABLE PROPERTIES / DATE OF VIEWING

Viewed
- ○
- ○
- ○
- ○
- ○
- ○
- ○
- ○

## NOTES

## PROPERTY SOLD | COSTS

| | Value | |
| --- | --- | --- |
| | Sold For | |
| | Commission | |
| | | |
| | | |
| | | |
| | | |
| | | |

# INDIVIDUAL REAL ESTATE LOG

| NAME: | | DATE: | |
|---|---|---|---|
| PHONE NUMBER: | | EMAIL: | |
| ADDRESS: | | | |

| BUDGET: | | DEPOSIT: | |
|---|---|---|---|

## PREFERRED LOCATION | PROPERTY NEEDS

| | | | |
|---|---|---|---|
| • | • | • | • |
| • | • | • | • |
| • | • | • | • |
| • | • | • | • |
| • | • | • | • |
| • | • | • | • |
| • | • | • | • |
| • | • | • | • |

## SUITABLE PROPERTIES

| Viewed | |
|---|---|
| ○ | |
| ○ | |
| ○ | |
| ○ | |
| ○ | |
| ○ | |
| ○ | |
| ○ | |

## NOTES

_____
_____
_____
_____
_____

## PROPERTY SOLD | COSTS

| | | |
|---|---|---|
| | Value | |
| | Sold For | |
| | Commission | |
| | | |
| | | |
| | | |
| | | |
| | | |

# INDIVIDUAL REAL ESTATE LOG

NAME: _____  DATE: _____

PHONE NUMBER: _____  EMAIL: _____

ADDRESS: _____

BUDGET: _____  DEPOSIT: _____

## PREFERRED LOCATION | PROPERTY NEEDS

- 
- 
- 
- 
- 
- 
- 
- 
- 

## SUITABLE PROPERTIES / DATE OF VIEWING

| Viewed | |
|--------|--|
| ○ | |
| ○ | |
| ○ | |
| ○ | |
| ○ | |
| ○ | |
| ○ | |
| ○ | |

## NOTES

_____
_____
_____
_____
_____

## PROPERTY SOLD | COSTS

| | Value | |
|--|-------|--|
| | Sold For | |
| | Commission | |
| | | |
| | | |
| | | |
| | | |

# INDIVIDUAL REAL ESTATE LOG

| NAME: | | DATE: | |
|---|---|---|---|
| PHONE NUMBER: | | EMAIL: | |
| ADDRESS: | | | |
| BUDGET: | | DEPOSIT: | |

## PREFERRED LOCATION | PROPERTY NEEDS

- 
- 
- 
- 
- 
- 
- 
- 
- 

## SUITABLE PROPERTIES

Viewed
- ○
- ○
- ○
- ○
- ○
- ○
- ○
- ○

## NOTES

_____
_____
_____
_____
_____
_____

## PROPERTY SOLD | COSTS

| | |
|---|---|
| Value | |
| Sold For | |
| Commission | |
| | |
| | |
| | |
| | |
| | |
| | |

# INDIVIDUAL REAL ESTATE LOG

**NAME:**  
**PHONE NUMBER:**  
**ADDRESS:**  

**DATE:**  
**EMAIL:**  

**BUDGET:**  
**DEPOSIT:**  

## PREFERRED LOCATION | PROPERTY NEEDS

- 
- 
- 
- 
- 
- 
- 
- 
- 

## SUITABLE PROPERTIES / DATE OF VIEWING

Viewed
- ○
- ○
- ○
- ○
- ○
- ○
- ○
- ○

## NOTES

## PROPERTY SOLD | COSTS

| | |
|---|---|
| Value | |
| Sold For | |
| Commission | |
| | |
| | |
| | |
| | |
| | |

# INDIVIDUAL REAL ESTATE LOG

| NAME: | | DATE: | |
|---|---|---|---|
| PHONE NUMBER: | | EMAIL: | |
| ADDRESS: | | | |
| BUDGET: | | DEPOSIT: | |

| PREFERRED LOCATION | | PROPERTY NEEDS | |
|---|---|---|---|
| • | • | • | • |
| • | • | • | • |
| • | • | • | • |
| • | • | • | • |
| • | • | • | • |
| • | • | • | • |
| • | • | • | • |
| • | • | • | • |

## SUITABLE PROPERTIES

| Viewed | |
|---|---|
| ○ | |
| ○ | |
| ○ | |
| ○ | |
| ○ | |
| ○ | |
| ○ | |
| ○ | |

## NOTES

_____
_____
_____
_____
_____

| PROPERTY SOLD | | COSTS |
|---|---|---|
| | Value | |
| | Sold For | |
| | Commission | |
| | | |
| | | |
| | | |
| | | |
| | | |

# INDIVIDUAL REAL ESTATE LOG

**NAME:**                                   **DATE:**

**PHONE NUMBER:**                  **EMAIL:**

**ADDRESS:**

**BUDGET:**                            **DEPOSIT:**

## PREFERRED LOCATION | PROPERTY NEEDS

| • | • | • | • |
|---|---|---|---|
| • | • | • | • |
| • | • | • | • |
| • | • | • | • |
| • | • | • | • |
| • | • | • | • |
| • | • | • | • |
| • | • | • | • |

## SUITABLE PROPERTIES / DATE OF VIEWING

| Viewed | |
|---|---|
| ○ | |
| ○ | |
| ○ | |
| ○ | |
| ○ | |
| ○ | |
| ○ | |
| ○ | |

## NOTES

## PROPERTY SOLD | COSTS

| | Value | |
|---|---|---|
| | Sold For | |
| | Commission | |
| | | |
| | | |
| | | |
| | | |

# INDIVIDUAL REAL ESTATE LOG

| NAME: | | DATE: | |
|---|---|---|---|
| PHONE NUMBER: | | EMAIL: | |
| ADDRESS: | | | |
| BUDGET: | | DEPOSIT: | |

| PREFERRED LOCATION | | PROPERTY NEEDS | |
|---|---|---|---|
| • | • | • | • |
| • | • | • | • |
| • | • | • | • |
| • | • | • | • |
| • | • | • | • |
| • | • | • | • |
| • | • | • | • |
| • | • | • | • |
| • | • | • | • |

## SUITABLE PROPERTIES

| Viewed | |
|---|---|
| ○ | |
| ○ | |
| ○ | |
| ○ | |
| ○ | |
| ○ | |
| ○ | |
| ○ | |
| ○ | |

## NOTES

_____
_____
_____
_____
_____

| PROPERTY SOLD | | COSTS | |
|---|---|---|---|
| | Value | | |
| | Sold For | | |
| | Commission | | |
| | | | |
| | | | |
| | | | |
| | | | |

# INDIVIDUAL REAL ESTATE LOG

**NAME:**  
**PHONE NUMBER:**  
**ADDRESS:**  

**DATE:**  
**EMAIL:**  

**BUDGET:**  **DEPOSIT:**

## PREFERRED LOCATION | PROPERTY NEEDS

- 
- 
- 
- 
- 
- 
- 
- 
- 

## SUITABLE PROPERTIES / DATE OF VIEWING

Viewed
- ○
- ○
- ○
- ○
- ○
- ○
- ○
- ○

## NOTES

## PROPERTY SOLD | COSTS

| | |
|---|---|
| Value | |
| Sold For | |
| Commission | |
| | |
| | |
| | |
| | |

# INDIVIDUAL REAL ESTATE LOG

| NAME: | | DATE: | |
|---|---|---|---|
| PHONE NUMBER: | | EMAIL: | |
| ADDRESS: | | | |
| BUDGET: | | DEPOSIT: | |

## PREFERRED LOCATION | PROPERTY NEEDS

- 
- 
- 
- 
- 
- 
- 
- 
- 

## SUITABLE PROPERTIES

Viewed
- ○
- ○
- ○
- ○
- ○
- ○
- ○
- ○

## NOTES

## PROPERTY SOLD | COSTS

| | Value | |
| --- | --- | --- |
| | Sold For | |
| | Commission | |

# INDIVIDUAL REAL ESTATE LOG

**NAME:** 
**DATE:** 
**PHONE NUMBER:** 
**EMAIL:** 
**ADDRESS:** 

**BUDGET:** 
**DEPOSIT:** 

## PREFERRED LOCATION | PROPERTY NEEDS

| PREFERRED LOCATION | | PROPERTY NEEDS | |
|---|---|---|---|
| • | • | • | • |
| • | • | • | • |
| • | • | • | • |
| • | • | • | • |
| • | • | • | • |
| • | • | • | • |
| • | • | • | • |
| • | • | • | • |

### SUITABLE PROPERTIES / DATE OF VIEWING

| Viewed | |
|---|---|
| ○ | |
| ○ | |
| ○ | |
| ○ | |
| ○ | |
| ○ | |
| ○ | |
| ○ | |

## NOTES

_____
_____
_____
_____
_____
_____

## PROPERTY SOLD | COSTS

| PROPERTY SOLD | | |
|---|---|---|
| | Value | |
| | Sold For | |
| | Commission | |
| | | |
| | | |
| | | |
| | | |

# INDIVIDUAL REAL ESTATE LOG

| NAME: | | DATE: | |
|---|---|---|---|
| PHONE NUMBER: | | EMAIL: | |
| ADDRESS: | | | |
| BUDGET: | | DEPOSIT: | |

## PREFERRED LOCATION | PROPERTY NEEDS

| | | | |
|---|---|---|---|
| • | • | • | • |
| • | • | • | • |
| • | • | • | • |
| • | • | • | • |
| • | • | • | • |
| • | • | • | • |
| • | • | • | • |
| • | • | • | • |

## SUITABLE PROPERTIES

| Viewed | |
|---|---|
| ○ | |
| ○ | |
| ○ | |
| ○ | |
| ○ | |
| ○ | |
| ○ | |
| ○ | |

## NOTES

_____
_____
_____
_____
_____

## PROPERTY SOLD | COSTS

| | | |
|---|---|---|
| | Value | |
| | Sold For | |
| | Commission | |
| | | |
| | | |
| | | |
| | | |
| | | |

# INDIVIDUAL REAL ESTATE LOG

| NAME: | | DATE: | |
|---|---|---|---|
| PHONE NUMBER: | | EMAIL: | |
| ADDRESS: | | | |
| BUDGET: | | DEPOSIT: | |

## PREFERRED LOCATION | PROPERTY NEEDS

- 
- 
- 
- 
- 
- 
- 
- 
- 

## SUITABLE PROPERTIES / DATE OF VIEWING

Viewed
- ○
- ○
- ○
- ○
- ○
- ○
- ○
- ○

## NOTES

_____
_____
_____
_____
_____
_____

## PROPERTY SOLD | COSTS

| | |
|---|---|
| Value | |
| Sold For | |
| Commission | |
| | |
| | |
| | |
| | |
| | |

# INDIVIDUAL REAL ESTATE LOG

| NAME: | | DATE: | |
|---|---|---|---|
| PHONE NUMBER: | | EMAIL: | |
| ADDRESS: | | | |

| BUDGET: | | DEPOSIT: | |
|---|---|---|---|

## PREFERRED LOCATION | PROPERTY NEEDS

- 
- 
- 
- 
- 
- 
- 
- 
- 

## SUITABLE PROPERTIES

Viewed
- ○
- ○
- ○
- ○
- ○
- ○
- ○
- ○

## NOTES

_____
_____
_____
_____
_____
_____

## PROPERTY SOLD | COSTS

| | Value | |
|---|---|---|
| | Sold For | |
| | Commission | |
| | | |
| | | |
| | | |
| | | |
| | | |

# INDIVIDUAL REAL ESTATE LOG

**NAME:** _____  **DATE:** _____

**PHONE NUMBER:** _____  **EMAIL:** _____

**ADDRESS:** _____

**BUDGET:** _____  **DEPOSIT:** _____

## PREFERRED LOCATION | PROPERTY NEEDS

| Preferred Location | | Property Needs | |
|---|---|---|---|
| • | • | • | • |
| • | • | • | • |
| • | • | • | • |
| • | • | • | • |
| • | • | • | • |
| • | • | • | • |
| • | • | • | • |
| • | • | • | • |

## SUITABLE PROPERTIES / DATE OF VIEWING

| Viewed | |
|---|---|
| ○ | |
| ○ | |
| ○ | |
| ○ | |
| ○ | |
| ○ | |
| ○ | |
| ○ | |

## NOTES

_____
_____
_____
_____
_____
_____

## PROPERTY SOLD | COSTS

| Property Sold | Value | Costs |
|---|---|---|
| | Value | |
| | Sold For | |
| | Commission | |
| | | |
| | | |
| | | |
| | | |
| | | |

# INDIVIDUAL REAL ESTATE LOG

| NAME: | | DATE: | |
|---|---|---|---|
| PHONE NUMBER: | | EMAIL: | |
| ADDRESS: | | | |

| BUDGET: | | DEPOSIT: | |
|---|---|---|---|

## PREFERRED LOCATION | PROPERTY NEEDS

| | | | |
|---|---|---|---|
| • | • | • | • |
| • | • | • | • |
| • | • | • | • |
| • | • | • | • |
| • | • | • | • |
| • | • | • | • |
| • | • | • | • |
| • | • | • | • |

## SUITABLE PROPERTIES

Viewed
- ○
- ○
- ○
- ○
- ○
- ○
- ○
- ○

## NOTES

_____
_____
_____
_____
_____
_____
_____

## PROPERTY SOLD | COSTS

| | | |
|---|---|---|
| | Value | |
| | Sold For | |
| | Commission | |
| | | |
| | | |
| | | |
| | | |
| | | |

# INDIVIDUAL REAL ESTATE LOG

**NAME:**  
**DATE:**  
**PHONE NUMBER:**  
**EMAIL:**  
**ADDRESS:**  

**BUDGET:**  
**DEPOSIT:**

## PREFERRED LOCATION | PROPERTY NEEDS

| PREFERRED LOCATION | | PROPERTY NEEDS | |
|---|---|---|---|
| • | • | • | • |
| • | • | • | • |
| • | • | • | • |
| • | • | • | • |
| • | • | • | • |
| • | • | • | • |
| • | • | • | • |
| • | • | • | • |

## SUITABLE PROPERTIES / DATE OF VIEWING

| Viewed | |
|---|---|
| ○ | |
| ○ | |
| ○ | |
| ○ | |
| ○ | |
| ○ | |
| ○ | |
| ○ | |

## NOTES

## PROPERTY SOLD | COSTS

| | Value | |
|---|---|---|
| | Sold For | |
| | Commission | |
| | | |
| | | |
| | | |
| | | |
| | | |

# INDIVIDUAL REAL ESTATE LOG

| NAME: | | DATE: | |
|---|---|---|---|
| PHONE NUMBER: | | EMAIL: | |
| ADDRESS: | | | |
| BUDGET: | | DEPOSIT: | |

## PREFERRED LOCATION | PROPERTY NEEDS

| | | | |
|---|---|---|---|
| • | • | • | • |
| • | • | • | • |
| • | • | • | • |
| • | • | • | • |
| • | • | • | • |
| • | • | • | • |
| • | • | • | • |
| • | • | • | • |

## SUITABLE PROPERTIES

Viewed
- ○
- ○
- ○
- ○
- ○
- ○
- ○
- ○

## NOTES

_____
_____
_____
_____
_____
_____

## PROPERTY SOLD | COSTS

| | Value | |
|---|---|---|
| | Sold For | |
| | Commission | |
| | | |
| | | |
| | | |
| | | |
| | | |

# INDIVIDUAL REAL ESTATE LOG

| NAME: | | DATE: | |
|---|---|---|---|
| PHONE NUMBER: | | EMAIL: | |
| ADDRESS: | | | |
| BUDGET: | | DEPOSIT: | |

## PREFERRED LOCATION | PROPERTY NEEDS

- 
- 
- 
- 
- 
- 
- 
- 

### SUITABLE PROPERTIES / DATE OF VIEWING

Viewed
- ○
- ○
- ○
- ○
- ○
- ○
- ○
- ○

## NOTES

_____
_____
_____
_____
_____

## PROPERTY SOLD | COSTS

| | Value | |
|---|---|---|
| | Sold For | |
| | Commission | |
| | | |
| | | |
| | | |
| | | |

# INDIVIDUAL REAL ESTATE LOG

| NAME: | | DATE: | |
|---|---|---|---|
| PHONE NUMBER: | | EMAIL: | |
| ADDRESS: | | | |
| BUDGET: | | DEPOSIT: | |

## PREFERRED LOCATION | PROPERTY NEEDS

- 
- 
- 
- 
- 
- 
- 
- 
- 

## SUITABLE PROPERTIES

Viewed
- ○
- ○
- ○
- ○
- ○
- ○
- ○
- ○

## NOTES

_____
_____
_____
_____
_____
_____

## PROPERTY SOLD | COSTS

| | Value | |
| | Sold For | |
| | Commission | |

# INDIVIDUAL REAL ESTATE LOG

**NAME:**  
**PHONE NUMBER:**  
**ADDRESS:**  

**DATE:**  
**EMAIL:**  

**BUDGET:**  
**DEPOSIT:**  

## PREFERRED LOCATION | PROPERTY NEEDS

- 
- 
- 
- 
- 
- 
- 
- 

## SUITABLE PROPERTIES / DATE OF VIEWING

Viewed
- ○
- ○
- ○
- ○
- ○
- ○
- ○
- ○

## NOTES

## PROPERTY SOLD | COSTS

| | |
|---|---|
| Value | |
| Sold For | |
| Commission | |
| | |
| | |
| | |
| | |

# INDIVIDUAL REAL ESTATE LOG

| NAME: | | DATE: | |
|---|---|---|---|
| PHONE NUMBER: | | EMAIL: | |
| ADDRESS: | | | |

| BUDGET: | | DEPOSIT: | |
|---|---|---|---|

## PREFERRED LOCATION | PROPERTY NEEDS

| | | | |
|---|---|---|---|
| • | • | • | • |
| • | • | • | • |
| • | • | • | • |
| • | • | • | • |
| • | • | • | • |
| • | • | • | • |
| • | • | • | • |
| • | • | • | • |

## SUITABLE PROPERTIES

Viewed
- ○
- ○
- ○
- ○
- ○
- ○
- ○
- ○

## NOTES

_____
_____
_____
_____
_____
_____
_____

## PROPERTY SOLD | COSTS

| | | |
|---|---|---|
| | Value | |
| | Sold For | |
| | Commission | |
| | | |
| | | |
| | | |
| | | |

# INDIVIDUAL REAL ESTATE LOG

NAME:             DATE:

PHONE NUMBER:        EMAIL:

ADDRESS:

BUDGET:            DEPOSIT:

## PREFERRED LOCATION | PROPERTY NEEDS

| PREFERRED LOCATION | | PROPERTY NEEDS | |
|---|---|---|---|
| • | • | • | • |
| • | • | • | • |
| • | • | • | • |
| • | • | • | • |
| • | • | • | • |
| • | • | • | • |
| • | • | • | • |
| • | • | • | • |

## SUITABLE PROPERTIES / DATE OF VIEWING

| Viewed | |
|---|---|
| ○ | |
| ○ | |
| ○ | |
| ○ | |
| ○ | |
| ○ | |
| ○ | |
| ○ | |

## NOTES

_____
_____
_____
_____
_____
_____

## PROPERTY SOLD | COSTS

| PROPERTY SOLD | | COSTS |
|---|---|---|
| | Value | |
| | Sold For | |
| | Commission | |
| | | |
| | | |
| | | |
| | | |

# INDIVIDUAL REAL ESTATE LOG

**NAME:**  
**DATE:**  
**PHONE NUMBER:**  
**EMAIL:**  
**ADDRESS:**  

**BUDGET:**  
**DEPOSIT:**  

## PREFERRED LOCATION | PROPERTY NEEDS

- 
- 
- 
- 
- 
- 
- 
- 
- 

## SUITABLE PROPERTIES

Viewed
- ○
- ○
- ○
- ○
- ○
- ○
- ○
- ○

## NOTES

_____
_____
_____
_____
_____

## PROPERTY SOLD | COSTS

| | |
|---|---|
| Value | |
| Sold For | |
| Commission | |
| | |
| | |
| | |
| | |
| | |

# INDIVIDUAL REAL ESTATE LOG

NAME:                             DATE:

PHONE NUMBER:            EMAIL:

ADDRESS:

BUDGET:                      DEPOSIT:

## PREFERRED LOCATION        PROPERTY NEEDS

- 
- 
- 
- 
- 
- 
- 
- 
- 

## SUITABLE PROPERTIES / DATE OF VIEWING

Viewed
- ○
- ○
- ○
- ○
- ○
- ○
- ○
- ○

## NOTES

## PROPERTY SOLD         COSTS

| | |
|---|---|
| Value | |
| Sold For | |
| Commission | |
| | |
| | |
| | |
| | |

# INDIVIDUAL REAL ESTATE LOG

**NAME:**                            **DATE:**

**PHONE NUMBER:**              **EMAIL:**

**ADDRESS:**

**BUDGET:**                         **DEPOSIT:**

## PREFERRED LOCATION | PROPERTY NEEDS

|  |  |  |  |
|---|---|---|---|
| • | • | • | • |
| • | • | • | • |
| • | • | • | • |
| • | • | • | • |
| • | • | • | • |
| • | • | • | • |
| • | • | • | • |
| • | • | • | • |

## SUITABLE PROPERTIES

Viewed
- ○
- ○
- ○
- ○
- ○
- ○
- ○
- ○

## NOTES

_____
_____
_____
_____
_____
_____

## PROPERTY SOLD | COSTS

| | Value | |
|---|---|---|
| | Sold For | |
| | Commission | |
| | | |
| | | |
| | | |
| | | |

# INDIVIDUAL REAL ESTATE LOG

| NAME: | | DATE: | |
|---|---|---|---|
| PHONE NUMBER: | | EMAIL: | |
| ADDRESS: | | | |
| BUDGET: | | DEPOSIT: | |

## PREFERRED LOCATION | PROPERTY NEEDS

- 
- 
- 
- 
- 
- 
- 
- 

## SUITABLE PROPERTIES / DATE OF VIEWING

Viewed
- ○
- ○
- ○
- ○
- ○
- ○
- ○
- ○

## NOTES

## PROPERTY SOLD | COSTS

| | |
|---|---|
| Value | |
| Sold For | |
| Commission | |
| | |
| | |
| | |
| | |
| | |

# INDIVIDUAL REAL ESTATE LOG

| NAME: | | DATE: | |
|---|---|---|---|
| PHONE NUMBER: | | EMAIL: | |
| ADDRESS: | | | |

| BUDGET: | | DEPOSIT: | |
|---|---|---|---|

## PREFERRED LOCATION | PROPERTY NEEDS

| | | | |
|---|---|---|---|
| • | • | • | • |
| • | • | • | • |
| • | • | • | • |
| • | • | • | • |
| • | • | • | • |
| • | • | • | • |
| • | • | • | • |
| • | • | • | • |

## SUITABLE PROPERTIES

Viewed
- ○
- ○
- ○
- ○
- ○
- ○
- ○
- ○

## NOTES

_____
_____
_____
_____
_____

## PROPERTY SOLD | COSTS

| | | |
|---|---|---|
| | Value | |
| | Sold For | |
| | Commission | |
| | | |
| | | |
| | | |
| | | |
| | | |

# INDIVIDUAL REAL ESTATE LOG

| NAME: | | DATE: | |
|---|---|---|---|
| PHONE NUMBER: | | EMAIL: | |
| ADDRESS: | | | |
| BUDGET: | | DEPOSIT: | |

## PREFERRED LOCATION | PROPERTY NEEDS

- 
- 
- 
- 
- 
- 
- 
- 

## SUITABLE PROPERTIES / DATE OF VIEWING

**Viewed**
- ○
- ○
- ○
- ○
- ○
- ○
- ○
- ○

## NOTES

## PROPERTY SOLD | COSTS

| | |
|---|---|
| Value | |
| Sold For | |
| Commission | |
| | |
| | |
| | |
| | |

# INDIVIDUAL REAL ESTATE LOG

**NAME:**  
**DATE:**  
**PHONE NUMBER:**  
**EMAIL:**  
**ADDRESS:**  

**BUDGET:**  
**DEPOSIT:**  

## PREFERRED LOCATION | PROPERTY NEEDS

- 
- 
- 
- 
- 
- 
- 
- 
- 

## SUITABLE PROPERTIES

Viewed:
- ○
- ○
- ○
- ○
- ○
- ○
- ○
- ○

## NOTES

## PROPERTY SOLD | COSTS

| | Value | |
| --- | --- | --- |
| | Sold For | |
| | Commission | |
| | | |
| | | |
| | | |
| | | |

# INDIVIDUAL REAL ESTATE LOG

**NAME:** 
**DATE:** 
**PHONE NUMBER:** 
**EMAIL:** 
**ADDRESS:** 

**BUDGET:** 
**DEPOSIT:** 

## PREFERRED LOCATION | PROPERTY NEEDS

- 
- 
- 
- 
- 
- 
- 
- 
- 

## SUITABLE PROPERTIES / DATE OF VIEWING

Viewed
- ○
- ○
- ○
- ○
- ○
- ○
- ○
- ○

## NOTES

## PROPERTY SOLD | COSTS

| | |
|---|---|
| Value | |
| Sold For | |
| Commission | |
| | |
| | |
| | |
| | |

# INDIVIDUAL REAL ESTATE LOG

| NAME: | | DATE: | |
|---|---|---|---|
| PHONE NUMBER: | | EMAIL: | |
| ADDRESS: | | | |

| BUDGET: | | DEPOSIT: | |
|---|---|---|---|

| PREFERRED LOCATION | | PROPERTY NEEDS | |
|---|---|---|---|
| • | • | • | • |
| • | • | • | • |
| • | • | • | • |
| • | • | • | • |
| • | • | • | • |
| • | • | • | • |
| • | • | • | • |
| • | • | • | • |
| • | • | • | • |

## SUITABLE PROPERTIES

| Viewed | |
|---|---|
| ○ | |
| ○ | |
| ○ | |
| ○ | |
| ○ | |
| ○ | |
| ○ | |
| ○ | |
| ○ | |

## NOTES

_____
_____
_____
_____
_____
_____

| PROPERTY SOLD | | COSTS | |
|---|---|---|---|
| | Value | | |
| | Sold For | | |
| | Commission | | |
| | | | |
| | | | |
| | | | |
| | | | |

# INDIVIDUAL REAL ESTATE LOG

**NAME:**  
**PHONE NUMBER:**  
**ADDRESS:**  

**DATE:**  
**EMAIL:**  

**BUDGET:**  
**DEPOSIT:**  

## PREFERRED LOCATION | PROPERTY NEEDS

- 
- 
- 
- 
- 
- 
- 
- 
- 

## SUITABLE PROPERTIES / DATE OF VIEWING

Viewed:
- ○
- ○
- ○
- ○
- ○
- ○
- ○
- ○

## NOTES

## PROPERTY SOLD | COSTS

| | |
|---|---|
| Value | |
| Sold For | |
| Commission | |
| | |
| | |
| | |
| | |
| | |

# INDIVIDUAL REAL ESTATE LOG

**NAME:**  
**DATE:**  
**PHONE NUMBER:**  
**EMAIL:**  
**ADDRESS:**  
**BUDGET:**  
**DEPOSIT:**

## PREFERRED LOCATION | PROPERTY NEEDS

## SUITABLE PROPERTIES

Viewed

## NOTES

## PROPERTY SOLD | COSTS

| | Value | |
| | Sold For | |
| | Commission | |

# INDIVIDUAL REAL ESTATE LOG

| NAME: | | DATE: | |
|---|---|---|---|
| PHONE NUMBER: | | EMAIL: | |
| ADDRESS: | | | |
| BUDGET: | | DEPOSIT: | |

## PREFERRED LOCATION | PROPERTY NEEDS

| | | | |
|---|---|---|---|
| • | • | • | • |
| • | • | • | • |
| • | • | • | • |
| • | • | • | • |
| • | • | • | • |
| • | • | • | • |
| • | • | • | • |
| • | • | • | • |

## SUITABLE PROPERTIES / DATE OF VIEWING

| Viewed | |
|---|---|
| ○ | |
| ○ | |
| ○ | |
| ○ | |
| ○ | |
| ○ | |
| ○ | |
| ○ | |

## NOTES

_____
_____
_____
_____
_____
_____

## PROPERTY SOLD | COSTS

| | Value | |
|---|---|---|
| | Sold For | |
| | Commission | |
| | | |
| | | |
| | | |
| | | |
| | | |

# INDIVIDUAL REAL ESTATE LOG

**NAME:**

**DATE:**

**PHONE NUMBER:**

**EMAIL:**

**ADDRESS:**

**BUDGET:**

**DEPOSIT:**

## PREFERRED LOCATION

- 
- 
- 
- 
- 
- 
- 
- 

## PROPERTY NEEDS

- 
- 
- 
- 
- 
- 
- 
- 

## SUITABLE PROPERTIES

| Viewed | |
|---|---|
| ○ | |
| ○ | |
| ○ | |
| ○ | |
| ○ | |
| ○ | |
| ○ | |
| ○ | |

## NOTES

_____
_____
_____
_____
_____
_____

## PROPERTY SOLD

## COSTS

| | |
|---|---|
| Value | |
| Sold For | |
| Commission | |
| | |
| | |
| | |
| | |

# INDIVIDUAL REAL ESTATE LOG

**NAME:**  
**DATE:**  
**PHONE NUMBER:**  
**EMAIL:**  
**ADDRESS:**  

**BUDGET:**  
**DEPOSIT:**

## PREFERRED LOCATION | PROPERTY NEEDS

- 
- 
- 
- 
- 
- 
- 
- 

## SUITABLE PROPERTIES / DATE OF VIEWING

Viewed
- ○
- ○
- ○
- ○
- ○
- ○
- ○
- ○

## NOTES

## PROPERTY SOLD | COSTS

| | Value | |
| --- | --- | --- |
| | Sold For | |
| | Commission | |

# INDIVIDUAL REAL ESTATE LOG

| NAME: | | DATE: | |
|---|---|---|---|
| PHONE NUMBER: | | EMAIL: | |
| ADDRESS: | | | |
| BUDGET: | | DEPOSIT: | |

## PREFERRED LOCATION | PROPERTY NEEDS

- 
- 
- 
- 
- 
- 
- 
- 
- 

## SUITABLE PROPERTIES

| Viewed | |
|---|---|
| ○ | |
| ○ | |
| ○ | |
| ○ | |
| ○ | |
| ○ | |
| ○ | |
| ○ | |
| ○ | |

## NOTES

_____
_____
_____
_____
_____
_____

## PROPERTY SOLD | COSTS

| | | |
|---|---|---|
| | Value | |
| | Sold For | |
| | Commission | |
| | | |
| | | |
| | | |
| | | |
| | | |

# INDIVIDUAL REAL ESTATE LOG

**NAME:**            **DATE:**

**PHONE NUMBER:**        **EMAIL:**

**ADDRESS:**

**BUDGET:**            **DEPOSIT:**

## PREFERRED LOCATION | PROPERTY NEEDS

- 
- 
- 
- 
- 
- 
- 
- 

## SUITABLE PROPERTIES / DATE OF VIEWING

Viewed
- ○
- ○
- ○
- ○
- ○
- ○
- ○
- ○

## NOTES

## PROPERTY SOLD | COSTS

| | |
|---|---|
| Value | |
| Sold For | |
| Commission | |
| | |
| | |
| | |
| | |

# INDIVIDUAL REAL ESTATE LOG

**NAME:** _____  **DATE:** _____

**PHONE NUMBER:** _____  **EMAIL:** _____

**ADDRESS:** _____

**BUDGET:** _____  **DEPOSIT:** _____

## PREFERRED LOCATION | PROPERTY NEEDS

| Preferred Location | | Property Needs | |
|---|---|---|---|
| • | • | • | • |
| • | • | • | • |
| • | • | • | • |
| • | • | • | • |
| • | • | • | • |
| • | • | • | • |
| • | • | • | • |
| • | • | • | • |

## SUITABLE PROPERTIES

| Viewed | |
|---|---|
| ○ | |
| ○ | |
| ○ | |
| ○ | |
| ○ | |
| ○ | |
| ○ | |
| ○ | |

## NOTES

_____
_____
_____
_____
_____
_____

## PROPERTY SOLD | COSTS

| Property Sold | | | |
|---|---|---|---|
| | Value | | |
| | Sold For | | |
| | Commission | | |
| | | | |
| | | | |
| | | | |
| | | | |

# INDIVIDUAL REAL ESTATE LOG

**NAME:** _____   **DATE:** _____

**PHONE NUMBER:** _____   **EMAIL:** _____

**ADDRESS:** _____

**BUDGET:** _____   **DEPOSIT:** _____

## PREFERRED LOCATION | PROPERTY NEEDS

- 
- 
- 
- 
- 
- 
- 
- 
- 

## SUITABLE PROPERTIES / DATE OF VIEWING

Viewed
- ○
- ○
- ○
- ○
- ○
- ○
- ○
- ○

## NOTES

_____
_____
_____
_____
_____
_____
_____

## PROPERTY SOLD | COSTS

| | |
|---|---|
| Value | |
| Sold For | |
| Commission | |
| | |
| | |
| | |
| | |

# INDIVIDUAL REAL ESTATE LOG

| NAME: | | DATE: | |
|---|---|---|---|
| PHONE NUMBER: | | EMAIL: | |
| ADDRESS: | | | |

| BUDGET: | | DEPOSIT: | |
|---|---|---|---|

## PREFERRED LOCATION | PROPERTY NEEDS

| | | | |
|---|---|---|---|
| • | • | • | • |
| • | • | • | • |
| • | • | • | • |
| • | • | • | • |
| • | • | • | • |
| • | • | • | • |
| • | • | • | • |
| • | • | • | • |
| • | • | • | • |

## SUITABLE PROPERTIES

| Viewed | |
|---|---|
| ○ | |
| ○ | |
| ○ | |
| ○ | |
| ○ | |
| ○ | |
| ○ | |
| ○ | |

## NOTES

_____
_____
_____
_____
_____

## PROPERTY SOLD | COSTS

| | | |
|---|---|---|
| | Value | |
| | Sold For | |
| | Commission | |
| | | |
| | | |
| | | |
| | | |

# INDIVIDUAL REAL ESTATE LOG

| NAME: | | DATE: | |
|---|---|---|---|
| PHONE NUMBER: | | EMAIL: | |
| ADDRESS: | | | |

| BUDGET: | | DEPOSIT: | |
|---|---|---|---|

## PREFERRED LOCATION | PROPERTY NEEDS

| | | | |
|---|---|---|---|
| • | • | • | • |
| • | • | • | • |
| • | • | • | • |
| • | • | • | • |
| • | • | • | • |
| • | • | • | • |
| • | • | • | • |
| • | • | • | • |
| • | • | • | • |

## SUITABLE PROPERTIES / DATE OF VIEWING

Viewed
- ○
- ○
- ○
- ○
- ○
- ○
- ○
- ○

## NOTES

_____
_____
_____
_____
_____
_____

## PROPERTY SOLD | COSTS

| | |
|---|---|
| Value | |
| Sold For | |
| Commission | |
| | |
| | |
| | |
| | |
| | |

# INDIVIDUAL REAL ESTATE LOG

NAME: _____    DATE: _____

PHONE NUMBER: _____    EMAIL: _____

ADDRESS: _____

BUDGET: _____    DEPOSIT: _____

## PREFERRED LOCATION | PROPERTY NEEDS

- 
- 
- 
- 
- 
- 
- 
- 
- 

## SUITABLE PROPERTIES

Viewed
- ○
- ○
- ○
- ○
- ○
- ○
- ○
- ○

## NOTES

_____
_____
_____
_____
_____
_____

## PROPERTY SOLD | COSTS

| | |
|---|---|
| Value | |
| Sold For | |
| Commission | |
| | |
| | |
| | |
| | |

# INDIVIDUAL REAL ESTATE LOG

| NAME: | | DATE: | |
|---|---|---|---|
| PHONE NUMBER: | | EMAIL: | |
| ADDRESS: | | | |

| BUDGET: | | DEPOSIT: | |
|---|---|---|---|

## PREFERRED LOCATION | PROPERTY NEEDS

| | | | |
|---|---|---|---|
| • | • | • | • |
| • | • | • | • |
| • | • | • | • |
| • | • | • | • |
| • | • | • | • |
| • | • | • | • |
| • | • | • | • |
| • | • | • | • |

## SUITABLE PROPERTIES / DATE OF VIEWING

Viewed
- ○
- ○
- ○
- ○
- ○
- ○
- ○
- ○

## NOTES

_____
_____
_____
_____
_____
_____

## PROPERTY SOLD | COSTS

| | | |
|---|---|---|
| | Value | |
| | Sold For | |
| | Commission | |
| | | |
| | | |
| | | |
| | | |
| | | |

# INDIVIDUAL REAL ESTATE LOG

| NAME: | | DATE: | |
|---|---|---|---|
| PHONE NUMBER: | | EMAIL: | |
| ADDRESS: | | | |

| BUDGET: | | DEPOSIT: | |
|---|---|---|---|

## PREFERRED LOCATION | PROPERTY NEEDS

- 
- 
- 
- 
- 
- 
- 
- 
- 

## SUITABLE PROPERTIES

Viewed
- ○
- ○
- ○
- ○
- ○
- ○
- ○
- ○

## NOTES

_____
_____
_____
_____
_____
_____
_____

## PROPERTY SOLD | COSTS

| | Value | |
|---|---|---|
| | Sold For | |
| | Commission | |
| | | |
| | | |
| | | |
| | | |

# INDIVIDUAL REAL ESTATE LOG

**NAME:**                                    **DATE:**

**PHONE NUMBER:**                  **EMAIL:**

**ADDRESS:**

**BUDGET:**                            **DEPOSIT:**

| PREFERRED LOCATION | | PROPERTY NEEDS | |
|---|---|---|---|
| • | • | • | • |
| • | • | • | • |
| • | • | • | • |
| • | • | • | • |
| • | • | • | • |
| • | • | • | • |
| • | • | • | • |
| • | • | • | • |

## SUITABLE PROPERTIES / DATE OF VIEWING

| Viewed | |
|---|---|
| ○ | |
| ○ | |
| ○ | |
| ○ | |
| ○ | |
| ○ | |
| ○ | |
| ○ | |

## NOTES

_____
_____
_____
_____
_____
_____

## PROPERTY SOLD / COSTS

| PROPERTY SOLD | | COSTS |
|---|---|---|
| | Value | |
| | Sold For | |
| | Commission | |
| | | |
| | | |
| | | |
| | | |
| | | |

## CALENDAR

| DATE | JANUARY |
|---|---|
| 1 | |
| 2 | |
| 3 | |
| 4 | |
| 5 | |
| 6 | |
| 7 | |
| 8 | |
| 9 | |
| 10 | |
| 11 | |
| 12 | |
| 13 | |
| 14 | |
| 15 | |
| 16 | |
| 17 | |
| 18 | |
| 19 | |
| 20 | |
| 21 | |
| 22 | |
| 23 | |
| 24 | |
| 25 | |
| 26 | |
| 27 | |
| 28 | |
| 29 | |
| 30 | |
| 31 | |

# CALENDAR

| DATE | FEBRUARY |
|---|---|
| 1 | |
| 2 | |
| 3 | |
| 4 | |
| 5 | |
| 6 | |
| 7 | |
| 8 | |
| 9 | |
| 10 | |
| 11 | |
| 12 | |
| 13 | |
| 14 | |
| 15 | |
| 16 | |
| 17 | |
| 18 | |
| 19 | |
| 20 | |
| 21 | |
| 22 | |
| 23 | |
| 24 | |
| 25 | |
| 26 | |
| 27 | |
| 28 | |
| 29 | |

# CALENDAR

| DATE | MARCH |
|---|---|
| 1 | |
| 2 | |
| 3 | |
| 4 | |
| 5 | |
| 6 | |
| 7 | |
| 8 | |
| 9 | |
| 10 | |
| 11 | |
| 12 | |
| 13 | |
| 14 | |
| 15 | |
| 16 | |
| 17 | |
| 18 | |
| 19 | |
| 20 | |
| 21 | |
| 22 | |
| 23 | |
| 24 | |
| 25 | |
| 26 | |
| 27 | |
| 28 | |
| 29 | |
| 30 | |
| 31 | |

# CALENDAR

| DATE | APRIL |
|---|---|
| 1 | |
| 2 | |
| 3 | |
| 4 | |
| 5 | |
| 6 | |
| 7 | |
| 8 | |
| 9 | |
| 10 | |
| 11 | |
| 12 | |
| 13 | |
| 14 | |
| 15 | |
| 16 | |
| 17 | |
| 18 | |
| 19 | |
| 20 | |
| 21 | |
| 22 | |
| 23 | |
| 24 | |
| 25 | |
| 26 | |
| 27 | |
| 28 | |
| 29 | |
| 30 | |

## CALENDAR

| DATE | MAY |
|------|-----|
| 1    |     |
| 2    |     |
| 3    |     |
| 4    |     |
| 5    |     |
| 6    |     |
| 7    |     |
| 8    |     |
| 9    |     |
| 10   |     |
| 11   |     |
| 12   |     |
| 13   |     |
| 14   |     |
| 15   |     |
| 16   |     |
| 17   |     |
| 18   |     |
| 19   |     |
| 20   |     |
| 21   |     |
| 22   |     |
| 23   |     |
| 24   |     |
| 25   |     |
| 26   |     |
| 27   |     |
| 28   |     |
| 29   |     |
| 30   |     |
| 31   |     |

# CALENDAR

| DATE | JUNE |
|---|---|
| 1 | |
| 2 | |
| 3 | |
| 4 | |
| 5 | |
| 6 | |
| 7 | |
| 8 | |
| 9 | |
| 10 | |
| 11 | |
| 12 | |
| 13 | |
| 14 | |
| 15 | |
| 16 | |
| 17 | |
| 18 | |
| 19 | |
| 20 | |
| 21 | |
| 22 | |
| 23 | |
| 24 | |
| 25 | |
| 26 | |
| 27 | |
| 28 | |
| 29 | |
| 30 | |

# CALENDAR

| DATE | JULY |
|------|------|
| 1 | |
| 2 | |
| 3 | |
| 4 | |
| 5 | |
| 6 | |
| 7 | |
| 8 | |
| 9 | |
| 10 | |
| 11 | |
| 12 | |
| 13 | |
| 14 | |
| 15 | |
| 16 | |
| 17 | |
| 18 | |
| 19 | |
| 20 | |
| 21 | |
| 22 | |
| 23 | |
| 24 | |
| 25 | |
| 26 | |
| 27 | |
| 28 | |
| 29 | |
| 30 | |
| 31 | |

# CALENDAR

| DATE | AUGUST |
|---|---|
| 1 | |
| 2 | |
| 3 | |
| 4 | |
| 5 | |
| 6 | |
| 7 | |
| 8 | |
| 9 | |
| 10 | |
| 11 | |
| 12 | |
| 13 | |
| 14 | |
| 15 | |
| 16 | |
| 17 | |
| 18 | |
| 19 | |
| 20 | |
| 21 | |
| 22 | |
| 23 | |
| 24 | |
| 25 | |
| 26 | |
| 27 | |
| 28 | |
| 29 | |
| 30 | |
| 31 | |

# CALENDAR

| DATE | SEPTEMBER |
|---|---|
| 1 | |
| 2 | |
| 3 | |
| 4 | |
| 5 | |
| 6 | |
| 7 | |
| 8 | |
| 9 | |
| 10 | |
| 11 | |
| 12 | |
| 13 | |
| 14 | |
| 15 | |
| 16 | |
| 17 | |
| 18 | |
| 19 | |
| 20 | |
| 21 | |
| 22 | |
| 23 | |
| 24 | |
| 25 | |
| 26 | |
| 27 | |
| 28 | |
| 29 | |
| 30 | |

# CALENDAR

## OCTOBER

| DATE |  |
|---|---|
| 1 | |
| 2 | |
| 3 | |
| 4 | |
| 5 | |
| 6 | |
| 7 | |
| 8 | |
| 9 | |
| 10 | |
| 11 | |
| 12 | |
| 13 | |
| 14 | |
| 15 | |
| 16 | |
| 17 | |
| 18 | |
| 19 | |
| 20 | |
| 21 | |
| 22 | |
| 23 | |
| 24 | |
| 25 | |
| 26 | |
| 27 | |
| 28 | |
| 29 | |
| 30 | |
| 31 | |

# CALENDAR

| DATE | NOVEMBER |
|---|---|
| 1 | |
| 2 | |
| 3 | |
| 4 | |
| 5 | |
| 6 | |
| 7 | |
| 8 | |
| 9 | |
| 10 | |
| 11 | |
| 12 | |
| 13 | |
| 14 | |
| 15 | |
| 16 | |
| 17 | |
| 18 | |
| 19 | |
| 20 | |
| 21 | |
| 22 | |
| 23 | |
| 24 | |
| 25 | |
| 26 | |
| 27 | |
| 28 | |
| 29 | |
| 30 | |

# CALENDAR

| DATE | DECEMBER |
|---|---|
| 1 | |
| 2 | |
| 3 | |
| 4 | |
| 5 | |
| 6 | |
| 7 | |
| 8 | |
| 9 | |
| 10 | |
| 11 | |
| 12 | |
| 13 | |
| 14 | |
| 15 | |
| 16 | |
| 17 | |
| 18 | |
| 19 | |
| 20 | |
| 21 | |
| 22 | |
| 23 | |
| 24 | |
| 25 | |
| 26 | |
| 27 | |
| 28 | |
| 29 | |
| 30 | |
| 31 | |

| CALENDAR | |
|---|---|
| DATE | JANUARY |
| 1 | |
| 2 | |
| 3 | |
| 4 | |
| 5 | |
| 6 | |
| 7 | |
| 8 | |
| 9 | |
| 10 | |
| 11 | |
| 12 | |
| 13 | |
| 14 | |
| 15 | |
| 16 | |
| 17 | |
| 18 | |
| 19 | |
| 20 | |
| 21 | |
| 22 | |
| 23 | |
| 24 | |
| 25 | |
| 26 | |
| 27 | |
| 28 | |
| 29 | |
| 30 | |
| 31 | |

# CALENDAR

| DATE | FEBRUARY |
|---|---|
| 1 | |
| 2 | |
| 3 | |
| 4 | |
| 5 | |
| 6 | |
| 7 | |
| 8 | |
| 9 | |
| 10 | |
| 11 | |
| 12 | |
| 13 | |
| 14 | |
| 15 | |
| 16 | |
| 17 | |
| 18 | |
| 19 | |
| 20 | |
| 21 | |
| 22 | |
| 23 | |
| 24 | |
| 25 | |
| 26 | |
| 27 | |
| 28 | |
| 29 | |

# CALENDAR

| DATE | MARCH |
|---|---|
| 1 | |
| 2 | |
| 3 | |
| 4 | |
| 5 | |
| 6 | |
| 7 | |
| 8 | |
| 9 | |
| 10 | |
| 11 | |
| 12 | |
| 13 | |
| 14 | |
| 15 | |
| 16 | |
| 17 | |
| 18 | |
| 19 | |
| 20 | |
| 21 | |
| 22 | |
| 23 | |
| 24 | |
| 25 | |
| 26 | |
| 27 | |
| 28 | |
| 29 | |
| 30 | |
| 31 | |

# CALENDAR

| DATE | APRIL |
|------|-------|
| 1    |       |
| 2    |       |
| 3    |       |
| 4    |       |
| 5    |       |
| 6    |       |
| 7    |       |
| 8    |       |
| 9    |       |
| 10   |       |
| 11   |       |
| 12   |       |
| 13   |       |
| 14   |       |
| 15   |       |
| 16   |       |
| 17   |       |
| 18   |       |
| 19   |       |
| 20   |       |
| 21   |       |
| 22   |       |
| 23   |       |
| 24   |       |
| 25   |       |
| 26   |       |
| 27   |       |
| 28   |       |
| 29   |       |
| 30   |       |

# CALENDAR

| DATE | MAY |
|---|---|
| 1 | |
| 2 | |
| 3 | |
| 4 | |
| 5 | |
| 6 | |
| 7 | |
| 8 | |
| 9 | |
| 10 | |
| 11 | |
| 12 | |
| 13 | |
| 14 | |
| 15 | |
| 16 | |
| 17 | |
| 18 | |
| 19 | |
| 20 | |
| 21 | |
| 22 | |
| 23 | |
| 24 | |
| 25 | |
| 26 | |
| 27 | |
| 28 | |
| 29 | |
| 30 | |
| 31 | |

# CALENDAR

| DATE | JUNE |
|------|------|
| 1 | |
| 2 | |
| 3 | |
| 4 | |
| 5 | |
| 6 | |
| 7 | |
| 8 | |
| 9 | |
| 10 | |
| 11 | |
| 12 | |
| 13 | |
| 14 | |
| 15 | |
| 16 | |
| 17 | |
| 18 | |
| 19 | |
| 20 | |
| 21 | |
| 22 | |
| 23 | |
| 24 | |
| 25 | |
| 26 | |
| 27 | |
| 28 | |
| 29 | |
| 30 | |

# CALENDAR

| DATE | JULY |
|---|---|
| 1 | |
| 2 | |
| 3 | |
| 4 | |
| 5 | |
| 6 | |
| 7 | |
| 8 | |
| 9 | |
| 10 | |
| 11 | |
| 12 | |
| 13 | |
| 14 | |
| 15 | |
| 16 | |
| 17 | |
| 18 | |
| 19 | |
| 20 | |
| 21 | |
| 22 | |
| 23 | |
| 24 | |
| 25 | |
| 26 | |
| 27 | |
| 28 | |
| 29 | |
| 30 | |
| 31 | |

# CALENDAR

| DATE | AUGUST |
|---|---|
| 1 | |
| 2 | |
| 3 | |
| 4 | |
| 5 | |
| 6 | |
| 7 | |
| 8 | |
| 9 | |
| 10 | |
| 11 | |
| 12 | |
| 13 | |
| 14 | |
| 15 | |
| 16 | |
| 17 | |
| 18 | |
| 19 | |
| 20 | |
| 21 | |
| 22 | |
| 23 | |
| 24 | |
| 25 | |
| 26 | |
| 27 | |
| 28 | |
| 29 | |
| 30 | |
| 31 | |

# CALENDAR

| DATE | SEPTEMBER |
|---|---|
| 1 | |
| 2 | |
| 3 | |
| 4 | |
| 5 | |
| 6 | |
| 7 | |
| 8 | |
| 9 | |
| 10 | |
| 11 | |
| 12 | |
| 13 | |
| 14 | |
| 15 | |
| 16 | |
| 17 | |
| 18 | |
| 19 | |
| 20 | |
| 21 | |
| 22 | |
| 23 | |
| 24 | |
| 25 | |
| 26 | |
| 27 | |
| 28 | |
| 29 | |
| 30 | |

# CALENDAR

| DATE | OCTOBER |
|---|---|
| 1 | |
| 2 | |
| 3 | |
| 4 | |
| 5 | |
| 6 | |
| 7 | |
| 8 | |
| 9 | |
| 10 | |
| 11 | |
| 12 | |
| 13 | |
| 14 | |
| 15 | |
| 16 | |
| 17 | |
| 18 | |
| 19 | |
| 20 | |
| 21 | |
| 22 | |
| 23 | |
| 24 | |
| 25 | |
| 26 | |
| 27 | |
| 28 | |
| 29 | |
| 30 | |
| 31 | |

# CALENDAR

| DATE | NOVEMBER |
|---|---|
| 1 | |
| 2 | |
| 3 | |
| 4 | |
| 5 | |
| 6 | |
| 7 | |
| 8 | |
| 9 | |
| 10 | |
| 11 | |
| 12 | |
| 13 | |
| 14 | |
| 15 | |
| 16 | |
| 17 | |
| 18 | |
| 19 | |
| 20 | |
| 21 | |
| 22 | |
| 23 | |
| 24 | |
| 25 | |
| 26 | |
| 27 | |
| 28 | |
| 29 | |
| 30 | |

# CALENDAR

| DATE | DECEMBER |
|------|----------|
| 1    |          |
| 2    |          |
| 3    |          |
| 4    |          |
| 5    |          |
| 6    |          |
| 7    |          |
| 8    |          |
| 9    |          |
| 10   |          |
| 11   |          |
| 12   |          |
| 13   |          |
| 14   |          |
| 15   |          |
| 16   |          |
| 17   |          |
| 18   |          |
| 19   |          |
| 20   |          |
| 21   |          |
| 22   |          |
| 23   |          |
| 24   |          |
| 25   |          |
| 26   |          |
| 27   |          |
| 28   |          |
| 29   |          |
| 30   |          |
| 31   |          |

Made in the USA
Lexington, KY
07 August 2019